This book belongs to

BASKETBALL
Players
2

B
S

GIRAFFE

let's
Go...

Hide & Seek

16
17

3

10

Beep..
Beep..

t
m

S

FUN
travel
Beep..
Beep..
Beep..

RACE
8
2

7
5

STOP
WAIT
GO

H
FIRE
RESCUE

Go...
5
5
M
7
7

??!
PaPa!!

tiger
go to
school

1 2 3
H

www.ingramcontent.com/pod-product-compliance
Lightning Source LLC
Chambersburg PA
CBHW080544060326
40690CB00022B/5209
9781679268427